Stop Worrying About Your Health

How To Stop Worrying About Symptoms and how Hypochondria and Health Anxiety Can Actually Make You Sick

James Umber

Copyright © 2015 SouthShore Publications

All rights reserved.

The advice in this book is not intended as medical advice. If you have any concerns about your health, you should seek professional medical advice immediately. Although the author and publisher have made every effort to ensure that the information in this book was correct at press time, the author and publisher do not assume and hereby disclaim any liability to any party for any loss, damage, or disruption caused by errors or omissions, whether such errors or omissions result from negligence, accident, or any other cause.

ISBN-13: 978-1517133153

ISBN-10: 1517133157

Claim Your Free E-book!

As a thank you for taking a look at this book I want to give you an e-book that is completely free right now! This book is not available on Amazon or anywhere else and is completely exclusive to my readers.

This book is called "Improve Your Personality – 8 Super Simple Personality Traits That Will Make People Instantly Like You"

This completely free book is so powerful because it will show you how to instantly boost your personality, which enables you to simultaneously improve your social life, your work life and your love life all in one go!

To get the free book right now, simply go to this link:

www.southshorepublications.com/improve-your-personality

The Other Books in my Book Series:

THE SECRETS OF SUCCESS & SELF IMPROVEMENT BOOK SERIES

Creative Visualization Techniques

Stop Caring What Others Think

Passive Income for Beginners

Find Your Passion

Self-Education

Stop Being Jealous and Insecure

Improve Your Conversations

CONTENTS

Introduction 9

Hypochondria 13

What is Hypochondria? 13

How Does This Affect You? 14

What Causes Hypochondria? 15

How Stress Affects You Body 18

A Quick Personal Example 18

Fight or Flight 20

Blood Pressure and Heart Stress 20

Immune System 21

Digestive System 21

Blood Sugar 22

Other Effects 22

Stop Overthinking Things 25

You Create Your Own Symptoms 25

Health Websites 26

How To Stop Overthinking Things 27

Accept and Realize 28

Breathe 28

Occupy Your Mind 29

Cognitive Behavioral Therapy 32

Why CBT is Great for Health Anxiety 32

Automatic Thoughts 34

The Underlying Assumptions 35

Thought Stopping 36

Give Yourself Cognitive Behavioral Therapy 37

Thinking Errors 40

Black and White Thinking 40

Exaggerating 41

Filtering Out the Positive Things 42

Emotional Reasoning 42

Fixing Thinking Errors 43

Things To Remember 46

Symptoms are Shared 46

Focus on Positive Thoughts 46

Don't Google Symptoms Ever Again 47

Check Your Thinking Errors 47

Final Thoughts 50

INTRODUCTION

Do you constantly worry about your health? Is your mood and everyday life dictated by the thought that there may be something medically wrong with you? Well, you're not alone. There are thousands of people going through the exact same thing as you.

I should know, I had to deal with this problem and I know how it feels to deal with this every single day of your life and live in fear, constantly worrying about some symptom or another. One day I decided that I had had enough and I sought out help. Now, I hardly worry about my health at all anymore. It's such an amazing feeling and I want you all to be able to feel exactly as I'm feeling now. I don't want another person to experience one more day of unnecessary stress and worry.

A hypochondriac is someone who has an abnormal or chronic anxiety about their health. If you can relate to the two chapters above, you're almost certainly suffer from some level of hypochondria. I did too. That was until I discovered the incredible information that I am going to relay to you over the course of this book.

I have also gained valuable insights and my own techniques along the way that worked better for me than those that others were teaching. This makes me ideally situated to write this book. Because not only am I going to put a whole plethora of tips, techniques and ideas all in one place, but I am going to also add my own personal tricks that I have developed along my personal journey and experience with health anxiety.

Rest assured that no matter what health issue it is that you're worrying about, the information in this book will be able to help you. Or even if you're like I was and you worry about multiple different health issues at the same time, what you are about to learn will help with that too.

Like I said, I've managed to stop worrying. If I can do it using the exact same techniques that I'm going to give you, all in one convenient package, then there is no reason why you can't do it too.

Another thing that you may not know is just how much stress really can have highly detrimental effects on your body. Stress can make you feel ill even when you weren't to begin with. You can also develop health problems and stress related illnesses just because you're worrying so much.

This is the ironic thing about hypochondria and heath anxiety. Even though you may have been perfectly healthy to begin with, just the fact that you are getting so stressed about your health, can actually make you ill. So it's of vital importance that we get this situation and your stress levels under control right away to limit and reverse any damage that your anxiety is doing to you.

Some of this information works really quickly too. There are techniques and mindsets that you can implement from day one to reduce your stress levels right away! So as soon as you have read this book, you can start feeling better right away. Don't worry, help is finally here and I'm going to guide you through every single step of the way on your road to a more enjoyable, stress free life.

Pretty soon, you will be living in a much carefree way with minimal stress levels. You will be able to enjoy the everyday thrill of living once again without any negative thoughts weighing down on you. So turn over the page and let's get started!

HYPOCHONDRIA

I wasn't lying when I said that you're not alone. It's estimated that around 5% of adults suffer from hypochondria. If you think about it, that's a lot of people. One in every twenty adults.

What is Hypochondria?

A hypochondriac is a person who worries about their health, even when the evidence tells them that they are healthy. They also tend to look for any tiny sign or minor symptom that may make them believe that they are ill when they're not.

These thoughts turn into much bigger issues in their head. The smallest thing usually gets blown out of proportion and turns into what this person could believe is a life threatening condition, even though it's not.

So you could interpret a perfectly normal bodily function as a serious health issue. Or if you have a minor health issue, you may start to worry too much and convince yourself that it could be a sign of something far worse.

Some hypochondriacs may routinely examine themselves for any small sign that they may have something wrong with them. To be honest, anyone doing this amount of searching and worrying is bound to find things that they could potentially worry about if they want to.

They may also do a lot of research online, which is a very bad idea for anyone in my opinion, even if you don't have any form of health anxiety. So for people like us, it's even more dangerous! No matter what symptoms you search on google these days, it usually comes back telling you it's something serious, even when it's not.

I have had friends who have done this kind of thing. For example, someone I know was waking up sweating every night and they googled it and found out that they could have something seriously wrong with them. They freaked out about it for a few days, thinking they were dying, then ended up finding out that their bedroom was too hot as someone had turned the radiator up by their bed.

How Does This Affect You?

Hypochondria can have a whole host of negative effects on your life. It' the same with any kind of stress or anxiety that is weighing on your mind, and health anxiety can be caused by plenty of things as you go about your day to day business.

It could be that you feel a pain in your stomach and that will set your mind racing wondering what it could be. This leads you to lose focus on other things and your mind is taken over by this strange pain and thoughts like, "What if it's something really serious?"

Even seeing an advert on television that shows someone with an illness can set a hypochondria off, even if you have no symptoms. Just seeing another person with an illness is enough to make many people with health anxiety think that they may have it or at least worry about whether they have it or not.

This can distract you from your job. If you're spending your working day worrying about health issues, you're not going to be able to focus on your work very well. It can stop you enjoying your leisure time because you can't stop thinking that you may have something wrong with you or that maybe you should go and see a doctor or get some tests done.

What Causes Hypochondria?

There are a number of factors that cause people to develop health anxiety issues. Some people are just natural worriers, although around 60% of hypochondriacs also have other anxiety problems or depression.

Your experiences in early life may also cause health anxiety. For example, abuse at a young age or having an illness as a child are both known to be contributing factors. Having a parent who has health anxiety can also cause the children to take on the parents habits and become a hypochondriac themselves.

Whatever the reason or cause, all health anxiety can be treated in the same way. Dealing with the issues that caused it, if the issues are extremely traumatic, can help for some people. But we are going to focus on dealing with what we are facing right now as this is the fastest way to put a stop to your damaging train of thought.

HOW STRESS AFFECTS YOU BODY

Stress can have a really serious impact on our bodies. So our anxiety and overthinking small problems, making them into bigger ones that don't even exist, can make us feel ill and develop new symptoms that we would otherwise not have experienced. This just serves to make things worse and give us new things to worry about.

So we really need to break this cycle of stress, worrying and anxiety about our health, which we will talk about later in the book. First though, you need to understand just how much stress can affect your body in order to realize the importance of breaking the cycle right away.

A Quick Personal Example

Just to illustrate my point, I have a very peculiar personal story that I want to share with you involving a something that happened to my father. He broke up with a long term girlfriend last year. Now, he doesn't deal with break ups very well and I could see he was really stressed about it. He was incredibly anxious that he would never find anyone new and that she was his final chance at love.

He basically blew it out of all proportion and made it out to be way worse than it actually was, just as us hypochondriacs do with our minor health related issues. Then after a couple of weeks of moping about, telling me that he was never going to find anyone new and stressing about it, all of his hair fell out!

I'm talking all of the hair on his head. It literally just started coming out in clumps for no apparent reason. He even lost his eyebrows! We couldn't believe it and we didn't know what was going on. Luckily he isn't a hypochondriac otherwise he would have been even more worried about it than he already was.

Turns out, it was just stress. The amount of worrying and overthinking that he was doing has actually caused his body to reject all of his hair. This is just an example of how much stress can have a huge effect on our bodies in very odd ways that we would not expect.

This is obviously not healthy and can cause our bodies to do some very strange things. This in turn will cause us to worry even more, and the stress cycle will just repeat itself and keep the problem going, week after week, month after month, year after year. So we need to knock it on the head now.

Just so you know, all of his hair grew back after a few months and he is absolutely fine now. This is probably due to him finding a new girlfriend and since he has been with her he hasn't had any more hair loss related issues.

Fight or Flight

When you experience stress, your body is in a heightened state of readiness. You have probably heard about this before, it's called the fight or flight mechanism and it's meant to get us ready to (obviously) either fight and deal with the danger, or run and try to get away from it.

So this system is only designed to deal with a threat and then shut off again once the situation is over. But if you're stressed, worried and anxious, this system stays on inside us for extended periods of time, which it's not meant to do. This can cause us some serious issues as my poor old dad found out the hard way!

Blood Pressure and Heart Stress

The fight of flight mechanism will cause our heart to speed up unnecessarily. This will cause your heart to work overtime in order to get blood to our muscles during times of anxiety. This in turn puts your blood pressure up as your heart is pumping your blood faster. Over extended periods of time, this can lead to heart attacks and heart disease.

High blood pressure can cause the cells in your blood to stick together more than usual. This can lead to blood clots which cause heart attacks and strokes.

Immune System

Just being stressed will cause your immune system to not work as effectively as it should do. Prolonged periods of stress and heightened flight or fight response will lead to decreased immunity in your body.

This is because when you are under stress, your immune system is suppressed. This means you are more likely to get ill more often and have even more symptoms that will cause you to stress even more! It really is a vicious cycle.

Digestive System

Similarly, your digestive system will also be suppressed. This is due to the same reason as your immune system. It's because the fight or flight response is diverting your blood flow to your muscles, where it assumes it's needed most. So less flow of blood to your digestive system means that it becomes suppressed.

This can lead to weight gain and obesity over extended periods of time, which can in turn cause a range of other health issues. Do you get acid reflux a lot? If so then this could be due to reduced digestive system function as a direct result of stress.

Blood Sugar

Surprisingly enough, stress actually increases your blood sugar levels. High blood sugar can lead to a whole host of issues including, diabetes, nerve damage and even vision problems.

Other Effects

Stress can also cause premature aging, a reduced sex drive, reduced sex function, infertility and a range of other issues too long to go into in this chapter!

Your body will also be flooded with stress hormones. This can lead to insomnia and a very disrupted sleep pattern, memory and concentration issues, addiction and depression. This is very common among people with health anxiety, especially the sleep issues.

So as you can see, stress is a really serious issue that we need to get under control as quickly as possible. Many of these problems only become an issue when stress is left unchecked for a very extended period of time, so as long as you take action on the advice that's to follow, you can help yourself avoid all of these problems.

Hopefully this information is all the inspiration you need to take action on the rest of the information that I'm going to provide you with in this book. It's so important to get your stress levels down, now that you have a better understanding of how it can lead to even more issues and symptoms that will only serve to cause us even more stress, you are ready to learn about how to resolve these issues.

STOP OVERTHINKING THINGS

The first thing you need to do when trying to overcome health anxiety is to stop overthinking every little pain or that little dry patch of skin, every time you get back ache or every time you have a headache.

You Create Your Own Symptoms

The mind is a very strange thing, it has the ability to create what we think about in the most mysterious ways. If you think about having a pain in your ankle, your mind will actually create that pain in your ankle and it will feel real.

Also things like worrying about having a high body temperature, will actually cause your body temperature to rise. So the more you worry about having certain symptoms, the more your body will create them.

Health Websites

This problem of creating your own symptoms is made FAR worse when you think you may have something wrong with you and you go and look up the symptoms online. Once you know the other symptoms that are related to something that you are worrying about, you will be on the lookout for them and you will begin to think about them. This often causes them to materialize even though you didn't have them already.

It's amazing how the information online can be so misleading. Many symptoms are shared by a whole host of different allergies, common illnesses and minor diseases that it's easy to convince yourself you have something far worse than you actually do.

Health websites and self-diagnosis websites are pretty much a hypochondriacs worst enemy. These sites put 2 and 2 together to get 5 million. They take the most basic, normal symptoms that are related to a whole variety of illnesses and lump them into one as they really have no idea what's wrong with you.

The main problem with this is that if there is a list of illnesses that are linked with the symptom you are looking up, you may see a really serious health problem on that list. You mind will instantly focus on the worst case scenario and you won't be able to get it out of your head. This will lead you to convince yourself that this very serious thing must be what you have wrong with you simply because you are overthinking it.

How To Stop Overthinking Things

Over-analyzing everyday occurrences and minor things, turning them into something they are not is common among all people who suffer from any kind of anxiety related issue.

Sometimes it's hard to get out of your own head and stop obsessing over a small issue, simply because you have made it into something much bigger than it really should be. This leads you to worry even more and it ends up going round and round in your mind, causing you to relate everything that happens to that one issue that you are focusing on. This process of overthinking can last months and even years if it's left unaddressed to float around in your mind.

If this is a common occurrence for you then you are a person that a psychologist would describe as a ruminator. This is essentially someone who lets thoughts run around in their mind and dwells on issues that cause them stress. This is more common in women than in men and it's highly detrimental to both your mental and physical health.

So, over the rest of this chapter I'm going to cover some techniques that you can use in order to help end this process and stop overthinking things.

Accept and Realize

The first step in overcoming the overthinking and overanalyzing process, as with many issues, is to simply realize you are doing it and accept that this is a serious problem for you.

You should also understand that it's only natural to think this way. The human mind is geared to combine negative thoughts and emotions and bundle them together. When one bad thought creeps in, it opens up the door to many others as our brains connects and links all negative thoughts. So don't blame yourself, just accept it.

You may see links that are not real simply because of the way your mind works. It instinctively tried to make sense of negative emotions by bringing up other negative thoughts that may or may not relate to what you're thinking. This can cause you to link them when they aren't supposed to be.

Breathe

There's a good reason why people tell you to breathe when you're stressed or feeling tense. Not only does it help you to clear you mind of problematic thoughts and therefore help on a psychological level, it also helps your body relax in a more physical way.

Deep, slow breathing increases CO_2 levels in your blood stream. This relaxes you and fights the flight of fight response to stress, which we definitely want to avoid, by calming the adrenal system. Try closing your eyes, breathing in through your nose and out through your mouth.

Occupy Your Mind

One of the main reasons people overthink things is because they have time to do so. A helpful technique for me in particular is to occupy my mind with something else. Overthinking things is near impossible when your mind is completely focused on another thought, topic or activity.

Even focusing your attention on a television show can take your mind off of your negative thoughts. Going out and being around other people will force you to engage with them and give you less time to dwell on your worries. Even playing a video game or one of those Facebook games will require focus and attention, which will mean you have less time to dedicate to overthinking things.

As I'm quite a driven person, I found the best way to take my mind off of any thoughts that were causing me unnecessary stress was to focus my mind on progressing with my business and getting to where I want to be in life. I think this is so effective because it places your mind in a positive and optimistic mindset as you are working towards something better for the future and improving your life.

Also I have found that doing something highly productive with my day helps me rest far better at night and helps my mind shut off. Since noticing this, I have found that other people are reporting the same thing. So not only will focusing your mind on being productive throughout the day help with keep your mind occupied, it will also help you shut off easier at night and relax.

COGNITIVE BEHAVIORAL THERAPY

Also called CBT, cognitive behavioral therapy is a way of learning how to cope with fear and deal with it in your mind so that in future, you will have the right mechanisms in place to deal with it.

Why CBT is Great for Health Anxiety

Consider this, are our lives and experiences based on what has actually happened? Or are they based on what we perceive? It's an interesting question in many ways.

Surely, unless we comprehend something, process it and turn it into something we perceive, then it's not something that can be an experience or an event in our lives. So our life is essentially how we perceive it and what we think is happening, rather than what is actually happening.

Most people will take this for granted and think that they see the truth because it's what they perceive to have definitely happened. But this perception is still created by your mind. Everything that you think is a product of your mind perceiving an event in a certain way. This is proved by the fact that everyone is different. Exactly the same event could happen to a group of different people and each of them will perceive it in a different way due to assumptions and automatic thoughts that are created by our minds.

If we can change these thoughts and the way they are generated then we can start to perceive things differently which, if you're a hypochondriac or if you have health anxiety, is what you really want to happen. Becoming aware of the thinking process and understanding why our thoughts are developed in a certain way will allow us to better understand that there is multiple ways of thinking about a certain event.

Seeing as CBT is based on our thoughts and how we are thinking about things, rather than being based on what is happening or has actually happened as most forms of therapy are, it makes it perfect for helping us see things is a more logical and realistic way.

This is the real issue here. It's the way we are thinking about things and blowing things out of proportion that is causing us problems. So most forms of therapy won't actually work seeing as nothing is happening and most of it is in our heads.

To put it another way, cognitive behavioral therapy focuses on beliefs rather than facts. So to use a non-health related example, let's say your father left when you were very young and that has caused you issues. Other forms of therapy would dictate that you have to deal with what happened, whereas cognitive behavioral therapy deals with how you think about what happened. So you can see how this will help with those of us with any form of anxiety, as that anxiety is caused by how we feel and how are minds are interpreting things.

Automatic Thoughts

So when you are undertaking cognitive behavioral therapy, you will need to make notes on all of your automatic thoughts about the topic in question. So let's say you suddenly feel a pain in your chest. You would need to record your immediate metal reaction to that sudden pain.

Would you instantly think that you're having a heart attack? Or would you think something far more rational like, "It's probably nothing and will go away in a couple of minutes."

By utilizing this thought tracking process, cognitive behavioral therapy can actually track the results of the person during the process in a very structured way. This provides real, tangible evidence on the persons progress which is another great benefit of CBT.

The Underlying Assumptions

After you know your automatic thoughts, you will need to dig a little bit deeper and drill down to why you are forming each of these thoughts automatically. It's not just as simple as, "Well that's just what I think" because there is reasoning behind your thought processes that lead you to the conclusion that you have arrived upon.

This really helped me realize when I was being irrational and it still does if I ever have little a bit of a relapse and start feeling some kind of health anxiety again. This is because, when you try to get down to the reason behind what you think and there's no real reasoning there, you will begin to understand just how silly these thoughts you are forming really are.

So for example, if you have that chest pain we talked about a moment ago and you instantly thought you were having a heart attack. You need to ask yourself, why did you think that? Because you know that chest pains are a warning sign of a heart attack would probably be your response. But does that really make any sense? Just because you have a chest pain that doesn't mean you're having a heart attack. It's just a chest pain, it could be caused by any number of things.

So why do you think that? Because you read online that a chest pain is a symptom of a heart attack probably. Well this shows us that because you read that information online, you are now linking the two. So the real reason that you thought you were having a heart attack is because you are finding things out, worrying about them and then as soon as something related to it is happening, you're linking them together in your head in a way that causes you to overreact.

So you can see how we can start to get to the underlying issues using this technique.

Thought Stopping

This is a really critical part of the cognitive behavioral therapy process. You need to stop these thoughts. Easier said than done right? Well there are a few techniques we can use to help.

As soon as you feel these thoughts developing, before you mate a note of the thought and try to drill down to the underlying assumptions behind it, you first need to cut the thought off as soon as possible.

Some people like to actually say "Stop" out loud as a verbal conformation that they are going to stop that thought there and then before it causes them stress and anxiety. Obviously if you're around other people or in a public place, this might look a bit strange, but if you're on your own it works well. Really be forceful with it and firmly tell yourself to stop.

Some people like to visualize a stop sign in their minds. This is a much more subtle way of doing things and it also gives your mind something to focus on other than the thought that is making you feel anxious.

Give Yourself Cognitive Behavioral Therapy

You can actually give yourself cognitive behavioral therapy and keep track of things all by yourself. This will save you a lot of money on seeking professional advice and I would highly recommend giving this a go before shelling out a lot of money when you can just do it from home.

Obviously, seeking professional help is always going to be the most effective option, as having a trained professionals guidance and experience to help you along your way is very valuable. So if this doesn't work for you, don't write it off as it really does work. Just seek some professional assistance instead.

So the first thing you will need to in order to start your own course of cognitive behavioral therapy is to stop your thoughts as I said. Do whatever it takes you to stop that harmful train of thought dead in its tracks.

Next, keep track of your automatic thoughts. As I explained, this will give you a great way of tracking your progress and looking back over time.

Then finally, delve into the underlying reasons why these thoughts are so automatic for you. Really try to understand why your automatic thoughts are there. There are reasons why, when something happens, you instantly perceive it in a certain way. If you find the underlying reasoning, you will be able to understand the irrational nature of your thoughts in future and cope with them in a much better way.

THINKING ERRORS

By using the techniques of cognitive behavioral therapy we are essentially going to minimize thinking errors. Thinking errors are ways in which we make mistakes in our thought process that lead us to form wrong or inaccurate perceptions. People who tend to have very bad opinions on a host of topics tend to have a lot of thinking errors in their thought process. So do people with anxiety about any aspect of life, including your health.

Black and White Thinking

A common error among people with health anxiety is thinking in black and white. There is pretty much always a range of middle ground to consider when thinking about something. Some people however will only consider the best and worst case scenarios.

For example, you have 1 symptom and you instantly think you have a life threatening disease. So you're either thinking that you're fine or you're dying essentially. It doesn't get more black and white than that!

Hopefully you can see when I put it like that, just how irrational that is. So you need to start considering all of the other possibilities in between. Is it something that might go away by itself in a couple of days? Are there a whole range of other things that this symptom could be caused by other than the worst case scenario? The answer is always going to be yes.

Exaggerating

Exaggerating is probably the most common thinking error out there. People just blow things out of proportion, especially when you start to worry about a health related issue.

It's similar to thinking in black and white. You will tend to start to imagine an end result that would be worse and worse until you get to the absolute worst case scenario possible and then you just end up worrying about something that you have created in your mind.

The hard part here is knowing when you're thinking at a realistic level and stopping yourself from exaggerating the problem in your head any further. As from that point onwards, this would become a thinking error.

To counter this downward spiral of exaggeration, you should ask yourself a few things when thinking about the issue in question. Ask yourself what the good signs are instead of focusing only on the negatives. Also, rather than asking the automatic and irrational question of, "What if the worst were to happen?" instead ask yourself the far more sensible question of, "What is the most likely thing to happen?"

Filtering Out the Positive Things

Sometimes there will be a lot of good things that reinforce the fact that we are perfectly healthy, then one bad thing happens and we just focus on and that filter out all of the good evidence. We may think we are sick, despite all of the contradictory evidence.

To combat this, you can write down a physical list on paper of all of the things that make you think you are ill and weigh them up against the things that make you think you are fine. When you write this down, your mind can't filter out the good points even if it wants to because it's written down right in front of your eyes, making it impossible to not weigh up both sides and consider the evidence in a more rational way.

Emotional Reasoning

This one is particularly potent when considering health issues because it often involves fear, and there's not much more scary than having poor health.

Emotional reasoning is where rational thought goes out of the window and you allow your emotions to take over your mind. So for example, you know it's a good idea to quit a job that you're miserable in and move on to something better, but you're scared about it, you stay in that unhappy job for years longer than you should do. This is because you're letting fear make your decisions for you, you're simply too scared to quit.

The same applies to health related anxiety. When you listen to your fear and anxiety relating to your health, you are letting your emotions form your reasoning. This is one of the fastest ways to blow everything out of proportion and come to a completely irrational conclusion.

Just because you're scared of something, you will naturally focus on it and bring it to the forefront of your mind every time anything remotely related to it comes up. You need to understand that this doesn't mean its true. It just means that you're thinking about it, that's all.

So when you feel this happening, just use the stop method that suits you best to stop the thought in its tracks and let the fear die down. Then you will be in a far better place to create a rational thought as opposed to one that is clouded by emotion.

Fixing Thinking Errors

In order to fix these thinking errors you must first accept that just because you perceive something, it doesn't make it true. You must accept that your thought processes are probably flawed and they are causing your anxiety.

You don't need to replace you thoughts with excessively rose tinted counterparts. If you do then you probably won't believe them yourself!

Just consider things in a more logical way. When you do this, you will realize that many of the thoughts you are forming around your health are black and white, exaggerated, focused on the negatives and based on your emotions and fears.

THINGS TO REMEMBER

So, now you have some great tools at your disposal that you can use to fight your health anxiety when it flares up. There's a fair bit to think about, so before we finish, I just want to reiterate the main points that you really need to remember.

Symptoms are Shared

Many of the symptoms for the diseases that you are worried about are also caused by many other common and easily treatable allergies, infections and things like the common cold. So try not to worry so much as the chances are, you have a very minor issue that simply shares symptoms with other, more serious issues.

Focus on Positive Thoughts

There are probably things that you can think about that contradict the fact that you have something wrong with you. For example, let's say that the disease you are worried about causes you to lose weight and you haven't lost any. Focus on that. Because if you haven't lost any weight then no matter how many of the other symptoms you are focusing on usually, that one simple fact should be enough to keep your anxiety levels down as long as you keep reminding yourself of it.

Don't Google Symptoms Ever Again

It's very important for those of us with health anxiety to stop looking up our symptoms online. As soon as you find out information about a disease and what the warnings signs are, thinking about them may cause your mind to create the symptoms even though you don't have anything wrong with you. The best thing for you to do is to simply know as little as possible about the symptoms. That way, your mind doesn't have the information that it needs to make minor issues into something worse.

Check Your Thinking Errors

Refer back to this book if you need to or make notes of the thinking errors I have listed. Then when you get anxious and start thinking that you may have something wrong with you, go through the thinking errors and scrutinize your thought process.

Before long, you will find out what thought errors from this list you personally make most often. Then you will find that whenever you do become anxious, which will be less and less often as you continuously prove yourself wrong, you will automatically recall the thinking errors that ease your stress the fastest.

FINAL THOUGHTS

Well that about wraps it up for this book! I hope you gained some useful information.

I have plenty of other books out about loads of topics surrounding Self Improvement and I will be putting my new books up for free trials every now and again. You can view all of my books by going to my Amazon Author page:

http://www.amazon.com/James-Umber/e/B00UXZNTB4/

Also, don't forget to go get my free book that is linked at the front of this book if you haven't already!

Thanks so much for taking an interest in my work and I hope to speak to you all again very soon!